T0088146

Hexes for
the Modern Age

Hexes for the Modern Age

CONTEMPORARY CURSES FOR THE PEOPLE WHO IRRITATE YOU THE MOST

VAL BRAINS

Skyhorse Publishing

Copyright © 2017 by Val Brains

All rights reserved. No part of this book may be reproduced in any manner without the express written consent of the publisher, except in the case of brief excerpts in critical reviews or articles. All inquiries should be addressed to Skyhorse Publishing, 307 West 36th Street, 11th Floor, New York, NY 10018.

Skyhorse Publishing books may be purchased in bulk at special discounts for sales promotion, corporate gifts, fund-raising, or educational purposes. Special editions can also be created to specifications. For details, contact the Special Sales Department, Skyhorse Publishing, 307 West 36th Street, 11th Floor, New York, NY 10018 or info@skyhorsepublishing.com.

Skyhorse® and Skyhorse Publishing® are registered trademarks of Skyhorse Publishing, Inc.®, a Delaware corporation.

Visit our website at www.skyhorsepublishing.com.
10 9 8 7 6 5 4 3 2 1

Library of Congress Cataloging-in-Publication Data is available on file.

Jacket design by Rain Saukas and Val Brains

Print ISBN: 978-1-5107-2182-1
Ebook ISBN: 978-1-5107-2183-8

Printed in China

Contents

Hexplanation

Modern times call for modern ways to make terrible things happen to people who irritate you. Out of this previously unmet need, as if from a beautiful Victorian fountain, has sprung *Hexes for the Modern Age*. It's full of embarrassing, debilitating, and shame-inducing spells, conveniently organized by category so you can inflict discomfort in a very specific area of your target's life. And, if you're not the hexer but instead the hexee, please enjoy a new set of things to feel increasingly paranoid about.

Love (or Lack Thereof)

May you find the perfect match on Tinder, only to discover that the last photo is him posing with a tiger.

May you keep running into people you met on dating sites IRL at the grocery store.

May you never get beyond a first date . . . with anyone ever.

May your only dating prospect in med school have the same name as your mom.

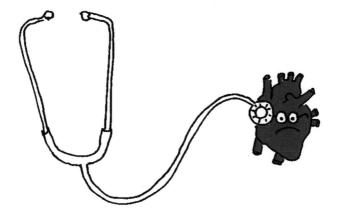

May a space in the community garden you've been on the waitlist for for two years finally open up . . . after you and your lady/man friend break up.

ROMANCE TIMELINE

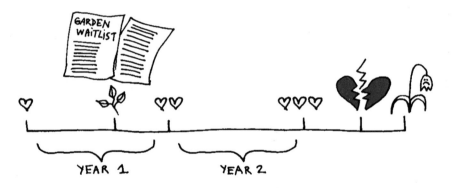

May your longest relationship be with your student loan debt.

May you run into the person you just went on a date with while you're on another date with someone else.

OPTIONS THAT ALL KIND OF SUCK

 PRETEND YOU DON'T SEE THEM

 AWKWARD WAVE & SMILE

 INTRODUCE USING WORDS LIKE "MY FRIEND"

May your morning fart slip out right before you make it out the door . . .

. . . and may the person you're trying not to fart in front of fail to pretend that they are still sleeping and didn't hear a thing.

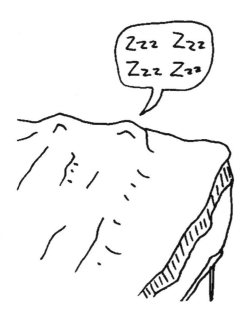

May you Tinder-match with someone from high school when you are home visiting your parents . . .

WAIT, WAS
THAT TIM
FROM HIGH
SCHOOL?

... and may they right-swipe you back.

IT'S A MATCH!

— OH SHIT.

May you drunk-dial your ex . . . again.

FRIDAY NIGHT + 🍸 + 🥫🥫 + 🍸 = *[phone screen:]*

FAVORITES

MD MOM

EX DO NOT CALL

SARAH

MC

May you mess up trying to give someone a fake phone number and accidentally give them your actual number.

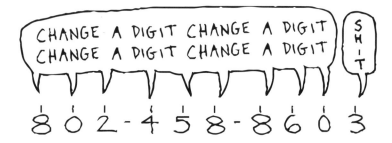

INTERNAL MONOLOGUE

CHANGE A DIGIT CHANGE A DIGIT
CHANGE A DIGIT CHANGE A DIGIT

SHIT

802-458-8603

May you both lack the courage to admit your attraction and may what could have been a beautiful relationship fizzle into nothing before it even begins.

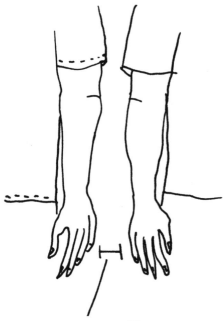

AMOUNT OF
COURAGE YOU LACK

May you continue to only get two out of three.

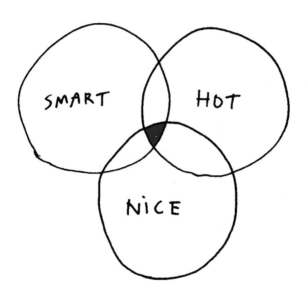

INSTRUCTIONS:
PLEASE CHOOSE TWO

SMART

HOT

NICE

Work, Work, Work, Work, Work

May you have two great interviews for a job you really want and then hear absolutely nothing.

May you work in an office dominated by the opposite sex such that it is always either way too cold or way too hot for you to be physically comfortable.

May you be about to leave the Friday before your vacation, check your email one last time, and receive an urgent last-minute project.

May you unwittingly hire the person who later takes your job.

May your weekly standup meeting be at 8:30 a.m., and may it be your only meeting of the day.

May you get stuck in the elevator with the coworker you most despise.

May you always be the one who yawns in a meeting.

MEETING TIME

YOU

EVERYONE ELSE

Pets

May all the plastic bags have holes in them when you run out of real dog-poop bags.

AVERAGE # OF HOLES PER
DOG-POOP SUBSTITUTE BAG: $2\frac{1}{3}$

May you step in dog poop in the shoes with the tiniest grooves, such that the poop is really hard to get out afterwards.

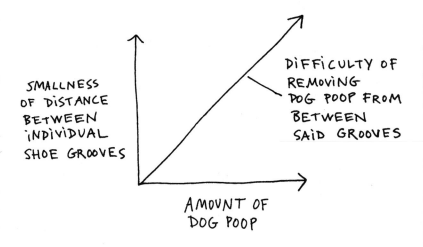

SMALLNESS OF DISTANCE BETWEEN INDIVIDUAL SHOE GROOVES

DIFFICULTY OF REMOVING DOG POOP FROM BETWEEN SAID GROOVES

AMOUNT OF DOG POOP

May you fall deeply in love with a cat person.

May you fall deeply in love with a dog person.

May the hot European guy at the dog park always be walking his girlfriend's dog (and may his girlfriend not be you).

May your dog openly despise your new boy/girl/dog/cat/pet friend.

May your cat throw up behind the couch, and may you run around wondering what that smell is for a week before you find it.

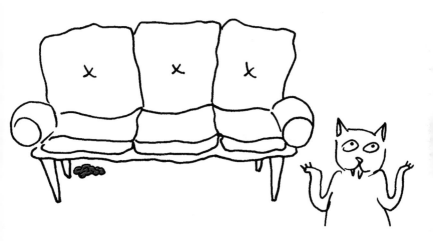

May your cat completely ignore the new scratching post you just bought for it and continue to destroy your furniture instead.

Family

May your father always be mistaken for your boyfriend when you're out in public together.

May your phone always ring during sex . . . and may it always be your mom calling.

May your mom always be right about everyone you date (and may you consequently remain single forever).

May your parents continue to ask when you're going to get married . . .

. . . and your grandparents when they can have some great-grandchildren.

May your much younger sibling reach all the important milestones before you do.

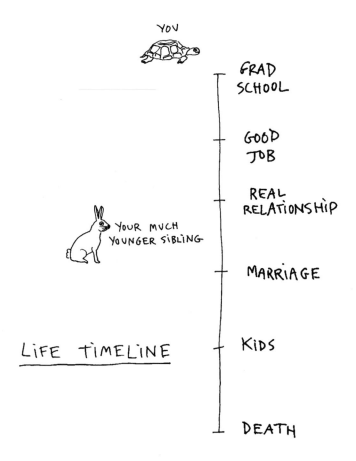

YOU

GRAD SCHOOL

GOOD JOB

REAL RELATIONSHIP

YOUR MUCH YOUNGER SIBLING

MARRIAGE

LIFE TIMELINE

KIDS

DEATH

May your mom interrupt the story you're trying to tell her with a bunch of questions about irrelevant facts.

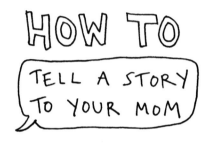

HOW TO

TELL A STORY
TO YOUR MOM

① BEGIN TO TELL STORY
② CROSS FINGERS
THAT SHE DOESN'T
ASK 10,000 QUESTIONS
③ GIVE UP & LEAVE ROOM

Driving

May you always have 3 percent phone battery when you have no idea where you're going and it's in the middle of nowhere and there's no one else around.

May you awaken to the blissful cacophony of a downpour . . .

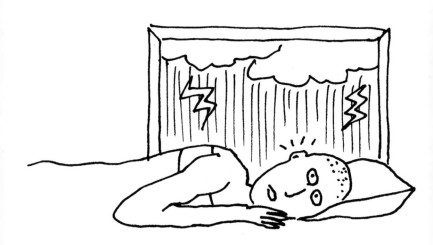

. . . only to realize you left your windows down.

May you always hear the sound of your car windows almost being able to close completely.

I SIZE OF WINDOW OPENING

SIZE OF NOISE

May a simple oil change always turn into $800 of repairs.

May every stop sign you encounter be the eternal stop sign of politeness where everyone arrives at roughly the same time and no one knows who should go first so you all just sit there for five minutes.

BEING
UNNECESSARILY
COURTEOUS

May you not be able to tell if the condensation is on the inside or the outside of the windshield.

NOPE

NOPE

NOPE

May a full-size parking space that appears to be open . . .

. . . actually be taken up by a tiny Vespa scooter.

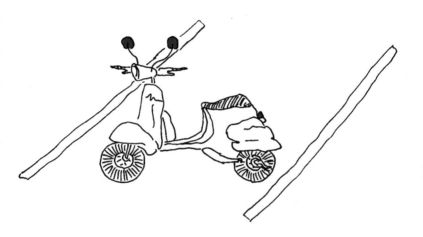

May you get a parking ticket for spending sixteen minutes in the fifteen-minute spot.

Hipster Life

May you never find the perfect shade of intentionally gray hair.

TOO GRAY

NOT GRAY ENOUGH

ALMOST THE RIGHT SHADE*

* BUT THERE'S STILL SOMETHING A LITTLE OFF AND I CAN'T QUITE PUT MY FINGER ON IT...

May your new felt Coachella hat blow away in a gust of wind . . .

. . . and subsequently be trampled into the ground by a bunch of people wearing boots worth more than your life in a cruel display of metaphor.

May the coffee shop bathroom toilet seat have a stranger's pee on it.

TOILET SEAT IN BUSY COFFEE SHOP

PEE THAT CAME OUT OF A PERSON YOU DON'T KNOW

May you always take the best pictures of other people while they take the absolute most troll-like ones of you.

PHOTOS OF YOU, TAKEN BY OTHER PEOPLE

May you make a day of going to Ikea only to find they're out of the sheets you wanted and you should have just ordered them online . . .

. . . and may you also come home with five other things you never intended to buy and don't actually need.

GEOMETRIC PRINT PILLOW

NON-DESCRIPT GLASS VASE

MODERN SCISSORS

ANOTHER SPATULA

TRAY FOR DONUTS

May all your moments of feeling just cool enough be extremely fleeting.

15 MINUTES LATER

Weddings & Events

May you find yourself seated at the singles' (read: misfits') table at every wedding with the expectation that you singlehandedly carry the conversation for hours.

May you be invited to ten weddings in the same year (five of which are destination weddings) when it's pretty clear you can barely afford to attend *one*.

WEDDING INVITATIONS HOLDER

May the ceremony be outside in the middle of the summer in a field with no trees.

May no one be able to correctly guess your Halloween costume.

SERIOUSLY??

May all those years of team sports lead you to accidentally catch the bouquet.

May no one laugh during the "funny" parts of your wedding toast.

May you always find yourself stuck behind a tall person at a concert.

WHAT SHORT PEOPLE SEE AT A CONCERT

May every photo of you at a summer wedding be you sweating through your suit jacket.

Getting Dressed

May you always find yourself on the wrong side of tasteful sideboob.

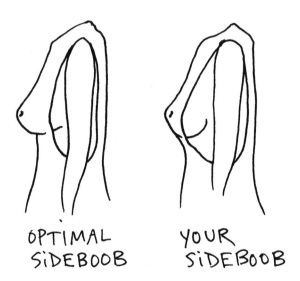

OPTIMAL
SIDEBOOB

YOUR
SIDEBOOB

May your nail polish chip before you make it home.

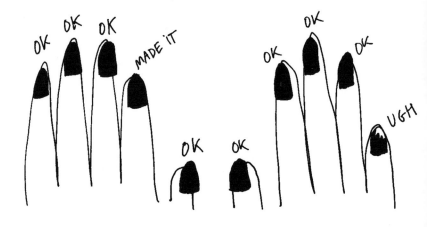

May all your yoga pants prove see-through.

May you sprout a toe hole in your favorite pair of socks.

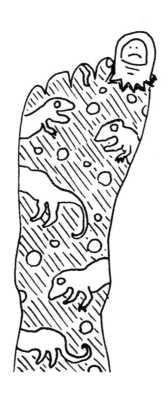

May you gleefully take out your favorite wool sweater for its first wear of the season, only to discover it's riddled with moth holes.

May you be deeply conflicted over whether or not it's time to throw out that old underwear.

May you go to buy a new pair of your favorite sneakers only to discover that they've been discontinued forever.

R.i.P.

2015-2016

Daily Drudgery

May you put something important in such a safe hiding place that you are then unable to find it.

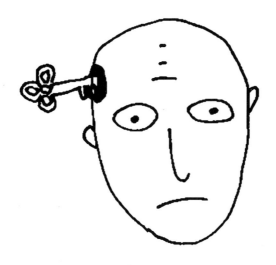

May you start turning into your parents way earlier than you expected.

May your horoscope always say that amazing things are coming . . . next month.

May you always get the neighbor's mail.

SWEET PACKAGE

DECLARATION OF LOVE

LETTER WITH A CHECK INSIDE

NOT FOR YOU

May you be unable to fall asleep because of that *one* mosquito in the room.

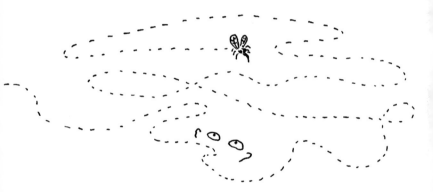

May you finally see Bigfoot and be unable to take a photo because your phone is out of space.

May you (and everyone you live with) forget to put the trash out.

Personal Hygiene

May you always miss a spot on the back of your thigh when shaving your legs.

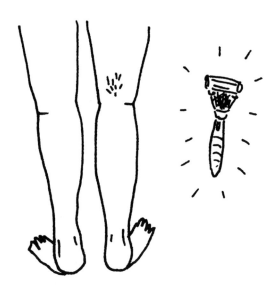

May you always forget to towel off your underboob.

UNDERBOOBS

RiRi'S   YOURS

May you always have a booger that you can feel every time you breathe in through your nose but that no one else can actually see.

WHAT IT FEELS LIKE THEY SEE

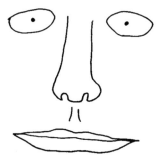

WHAT THEY ACTUALLY SEE

May your toilet paper never show clean.

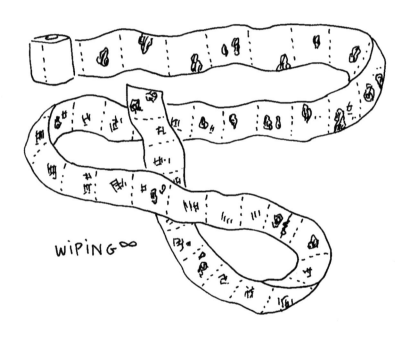

WIPING∞

May there always be something in your teeth that no one has the decency to tell you about.

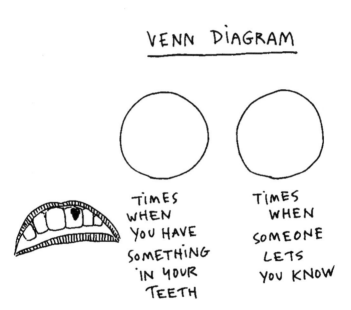

VENN DIAGRAM

TIMES WHEN YOU HAVE SOMETHING IN YOUR TEETH

TIMES WHEN SOMEONE LETS YOU KNOW

NOTE: VENN DIAGRAMS ARE SUPPOSED TO OVERLAP

May every important and photograph-able occasion be heralded by a giant zit appearing on your face.

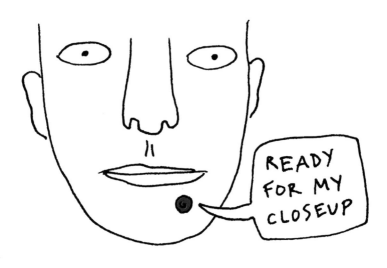

May you contract mono as an adult and be unable to explain where it came from.

COMMON SOURCES OF MONO:

- TEENAGERS
- MAKING OUT WITH TEENAGERS
- SHARING DRINKS WITH TEENAGERS
- BEING IN HIGH SCHOOL

May you run out of TP in a public restroom . . .

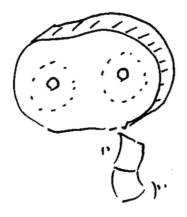

. . . and may you be alone.

May the soap have one lone pube on it.

PUBES: 1
SOAP: Ø

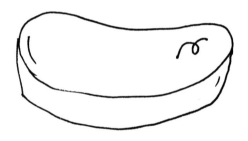

Roommates

May your roommate take your stuff out of the dryer and put it on a surface just dirty enough for you to have to wash it again.

ACCEPTABLE PLACES TO PUT CLEAN LAUNDRY

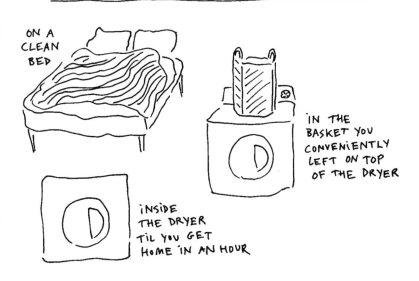

ON A CLEAN BED

IN THE BASKET YOU CONVENIENTLY LEFT ON TOP OF THE DRYER

INSIDE THE DRYER TIL YOU GET HOME IN AN HOUR

May your roommate always use the last of the toilet paper and never put a new roll on.

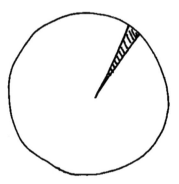

TOILET PAPER
ROLL REPLACEMENT
PIE CHART

May the loudness of your roommate's sexual escapades be matched only by their complete obliviousness.

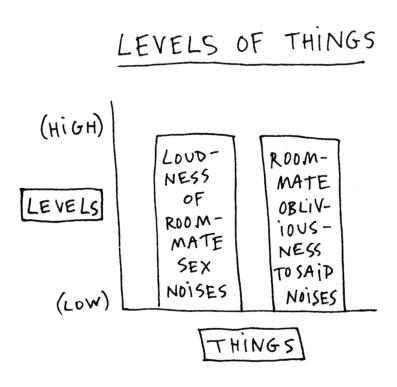

LEVELS OF THINGS

(HIGH)

LEVELS

LOUD-NESS OF ROOM-MATE SEX NOISES

ROOM-MATE OBLIV-IOUS-NESS TO SAID NOISES

(LOW)

THINGS

May your roommate always put things back in the most random-ass places when they unload the dishwasher . . .

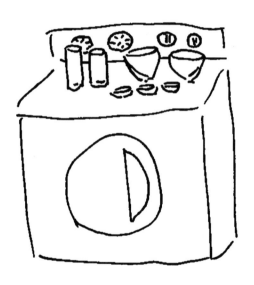

. . . and may you always wonder if they just do that on purpose so they don't ever have to unload the dishwasher.

HOW TO AVOID ROOMMATE CHORE DUTIES

ROOMMATE'S NIGHTSTAND

May you find toenail clippings that are definitely not yours.

May you be the only one home when the hair in the shower drain finally clogs the pipes.

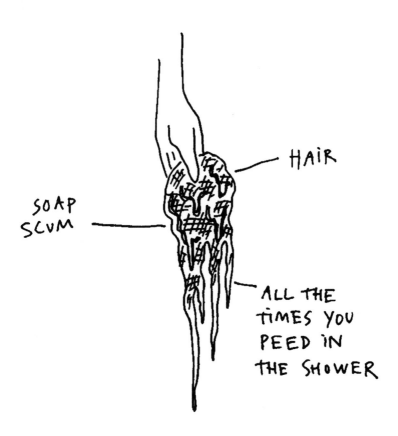

HAIR

SOAP SCUM

ALL THE TIMES YOU PEED IN THE SHOWER

Food

May you mistake the salt for sugar.

May you never be able to tell if the milk has gone bad until after you've poured it on your last remaining bit of cereal.

May the new restaurant be out of the very thing you went there to try.

May you wake up with eternal garlic fingers.

May you only buy one avocado, and may it turn out to be rotten.

	OUTSIDE	INSIDE
GOOD AVOCADO		
BAD AVOCADO		

May the noodle shop screw up your order but you be too nice to say anything about it and be forced to half-enjoy your half-right order.

DEFINITELY
MEAT

VEGETARIAN
NOODLE BOWL

May you always pull the popcorn flavor jelly bean.

BUTTERED
POPCORN —

ALL THE
OTHER
FLAVORS IT
COULD'VE BEEN

May all the muffins be vegan.

Travel

May you continue to find sand in strange places weeks after your vacation.

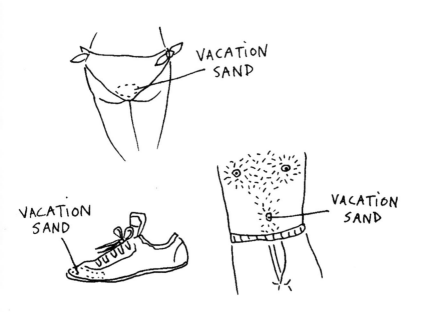

VACATION SAND

VACATION SAND

VACATION SAND

May you remember to pack everything . . . except your phone charger and underwear.

May you accidentally book your flight for the wrong month and only discover this when you get the "time to check in" email.

May you watch in dismay as your Uber goes in the wrong direction on the little map and you get closer to missing your flight.

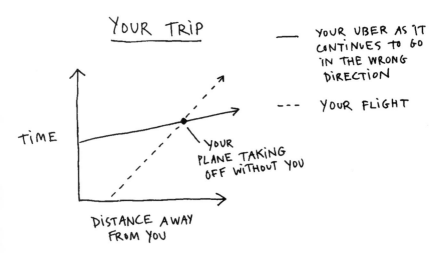

YOUR TRIP

— YOUR UBER AS IT CONTINUES TO GO IN THE WRONG DIRECTION

- - - YOUR FLIGHT

TIME

YOUR PLANE TAKING OFF WITHOUT YOU

DISTANCE AWAY FROM YOU

May you always have to take the express train one stop further and backtrack on the local.

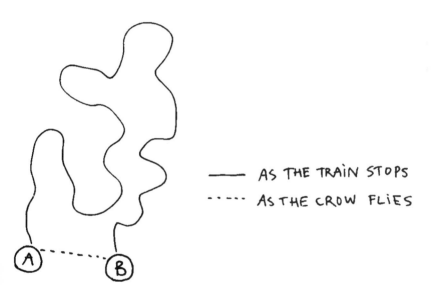

——— AS THE TRAIN STOPS

----- AS THE CROW FLIES

May your airplane seat neighbor use both of the elbow rests (without asking, of course).

May you always get "selected" for extra screening.

Technology

May you forget your brother's Netflix password, and may he not respond to your frantic texts about it for, like, twenty minutes.

May Siri always autocorrect the f-word to "duck."

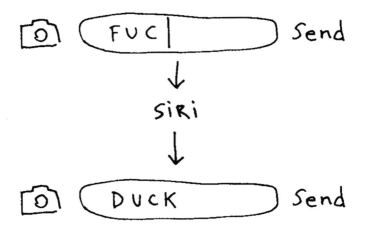

May you regret ordering that iced mocha after you spill it all over your computer.

May you accidentally delete the Excel spreadsheet that contains all your passwords because you are a Luddite and refuse to use a password encryption service.

May Siri never understand what you are trying to say.

May someone ask you to fax something and actually be serious.

May all the cords to your electronics become entangled in a massive death coil.

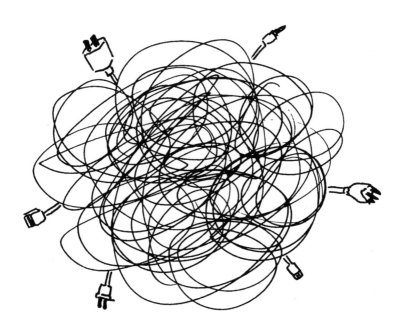

May you watch the three dots for like two minutes only to have them disappear permanently.

ALL OF THE EMOTIONS

May you accidentally send a topless selfie to your dad.

May you not figure out the undo extension for Gmail until it's way, way, way too late.

May you accidentally AirDrop a selfie on a stranger's computer.